Dedicated

to

Mizo Society and Culture

MATHEMATICS AND MIZO CULTURE

ETHNOMATHEMATICAL PERSPECTIVES ON CULTURALLY RESPONSIVE LEARNING

DR. PRATEEK CHAURASIA
& TBC LALRAMNGHAKA

Made with ♥ on the Notion Press Platform
www.notionpress.com

Contents

Contents

Contents

Foreword

We hope that this work serves as a testament to the invaluable contributions of indigenous knowledge systems to the broader landscape of mathematics education and research. As authors, researchers, and educators, our aim is not only to elucidate the mathematical intricacies of Mizo culture but also to spark curiosity, inspire inquiry, and foster a deeper appreciation for the mathematical heritage of indigenous peoples worldwide. Through our exploration of ethnomathematics, we hope to contribute to a more inclusive and culturally responsive approach to mathematics education, one that honors the diverse mathematical traditions of all peoples. May this book inspire readers to embrace the cultural diversity of mathematics, fostering a deeper appreciation for the myriad ways in which mathematical knowledge is created, shared, and celebrated across the globe.

Prateek Chaurasia & TBC Lalramnghaka

ϷϷϷ

Preface

In the vibrant tapestry of human knowledge, the threads of culture and mathematics are intricately woven, forming patterns that reflect the rich diversity of our world. Within this intricate design lies the essence of ethnomathematics – a field that explores the mathematical practices and concepts embedded within various cultures, illuminating the deep connections between mathematics and human societies. In the pursuit of understanding mathematics, we often find ourselves drawn to explore its manifestations in diverse cultures, seeking to uncover the intricate ways in which mathematical concepts are woven into the fabric of everyday life. It is within this context of cultural richness and mathematical inquiry that this book emerges – a journey into the fascinating realm of mathematics learning among the Mizo tribe.

Nestled in the verdant hills of northeastern India, the Mizo people have cultivated a rich mathematical heritage reflecting their deep connection to the land, traditions, and way of life. Yet, despite the wealth of mathematical knowledge embedded within Mizo culture, there exists a gap in our understanding of how mathematics is learned, transmitted, and utilized within this vibrant community. In this book, we embark on a journey into the heart of Mizo culture, a journey that reveals the profound mathematical wisdom interwoven with the fabric of everyday life. The Mizo people, with their centuries-old traditions and resilient spirit, have developed a unique mathematical heritage that reflects their close relationship with the natural world, their agricultural practices, and their social structures. Drawing upon the principles of ethnomathematics, this book seeks to bridge this gap by offering a comprehensive exploration of mathematics learning among the Mizo tribe.

Through a combination of ethnographic research, mathematical analysis, and educational insights, we delve into the unique pedagogical practices, cultural contexts, and cognitive processes that shape the mathematical experiences of Mizo learners. From the rhythmic chants of traditional songs that encode mathematical patterns to the practical applications of geometry in weaving and architecture, we uncover the myriad ways in which mathematics is integrated into the daily lives and cultural practices of the Mizo people. Through engaging narratives, illustrative examples, and reflective analyses, we aim to illuminate the richness and complexity of Mizo mathematics learning, offering valuable insights for educators, researchers, and policymakers alike. This book is more than a mere academic endeavor; it is a tribute to the resilience, creativity, and ingenuity of the Mizo tribe, whose mathematical traditions have endured through generations of change and adaptation.

Acknowledgements

The present book of Mathematics Learning in Mizo Culture is the output of research work based on the ethnomathematical study of Mizo Culture. The study deliberately explores the various components of Mizo culture and its intercept in teaching mathematics at the school level. The identification and elaboration of various components of Mizo culture are done with the help of surveys and interaction with local people, we are extremely thankful to local people who have contributed to the listing and identification of items of Mizo culture. We express our heartfelt and special thanks to Mizoram University, Aizawl, Mizoram for providing all the necessary facilities for the smooth and successful completion of this conduct.

ϸϸϸ

Prologue

The book is written on the principles of the National Educational Policy (NEP)- 2020. The prime idea of the book is based on the recommendation of the NEP-2020 to localize the content of the book. The present book lies on the background of the ethnomathematics, it tries to explore the indigenous material of Mizo culture and their intercept in the teaching-learning of mathematics. The book comprised a total of 50 indigenous materials. It contains a detailed analysis of the material concerning their pedagogical analysis suitable for teachers and students for mathematics learning. The book also covers the research outline and support of mathematics learning and its relation to the cultural aspect.

ONE

ABOUT MIZORAM

About Mizoram

Mizoram (Land of the Mizo people) is one of the seven sister states of Arunachal Pradesh, Assam, Meghalaya, Manipur, Mizoram, Nagaland, and Tripura in the Northeastern part of India. It is bounded by Myanmar (Burma) to the east and south, Bangladesh to the west, Tripura to the northwest, Assam to the north, and Manipur to the northeast. The capital is Aizawl, in the north-central part of the state. Mizoram "Land of the Mizos" was known as the Lushai Hills District of Assam before it was renamed the Mizo Hills District in 1954. In 1972 it became a centrally administered union territory under the name of Mizoram, and in 1987 it achieved statehood and has an Area of 8,139 square miles (21,081 square km).

The native people of the state are called Mizos, meaning the highlanders. Historians believe that the Mizos are a part of the great wave of the Mongolian race spilling over into eastern and southern India centuries ago. Their sojourn in Western Burma, into which they eventually around the seventh century, is estimated to last about two centuries. They came under the influence of the British Missionaries in the 9th century, and now most of the Mizos are Christians. One of the beneficial results of Missionary activities was the spread of education. The missionaries introduced the Roman script for the Mizo language and formal education. The Mizos area was a distinct community and the social unit was the village. Around it revolved the life of a Mizo. Mizo Village is usually set on the top of a hill with the chief's house at the centre and the bachelor's dormitory called Zawlbuk, prominently. In a way, the focal point in the village was the Zawlbuk where all the young bachelors of the village slept. Zawlbuk was the training ground, and indeed, the cradle wherein the Mizo youth was shaped into a responsible adult member of the society. The fabric of social life in the Mizo society has undergone tremendous changes over the years. Before the British moved into the hills, for all practical purposes the village and the clan formed units of Mizo society. The Mizo code of ethics or Dharma moved around 'Tlawmngaihna", an untranslatable term meaning on the part of everyone to be hospitable, kind, unselfish, and helpful to others. Tlawmngaihna to Mizo stands for the compelling moral force that finds expression in self-sacrifice for the service of others. The old belief, Pathian is still used in the term God till today.

The Mizos are a close-knit society who believes in love and harmony. Ninety percent of Mizo's are cultivators and the village exists like a big family. The birth of a child, marriage in the village, death of a person in the village, or a community feast arranged by a member of the village are important occasions in which the whole village is involved.

The Government's attention to education increased significantly after independence. Earlier the efforts were mainly to increase primary education. Quite several primary schools were gradually upgraded to middle and high school levels. The number of educational institutions is keeping pace with the thirst of the Mizos for formal education. The state also has different training cum production centers. It covers courses such as silk spinning and weaving, cotton spinning and weaving, soap making, oil extraction, carpentry, cane, and bamboo works, etc.

Mizo art and craft items are worth treasuring. Mizo women are born weavers and the intricate designs created by them are a treat to the eyes. The choice of bright colors in everything is a unique feature of Mizo arts and crafts. Innovative designs mark the exclusive cane and bamboo furniture of Mizoram.

TWO
MATHEMATICS AND CULTURE

Introduction

Mathematics and civilizations have a deep relationship between them. As civilizations have flourished, mathematics has also grown side by side. The evolution of mathematics is intensely related to various cultures. Ethnomathematics is the study of mathematical ideas that are embedded in the culture and literally in the daily life of an individual. Recognizing the mathematical thoughts notions and symbolic representation corresponds to the daily life of an individual.

The general mathematical ideas within a human being are developed under the effect of the experiences around them. National Curriculum Framework (NCF) -2005 advocates it as the mathematisation of a child. To make mathematics linked with the daily life of the learners has been the prime concern of the stakeholders of mathematics teaching. Ethnomathematics plays the role of cantilever between formal concepts and visualizing their practice in a culture so that students' understanding becomes more concretized due to its direct linkage with the culture, which is the inevitable daily practice of the individual's activity.

Ethnomathematics aims to recognize different ways of expressing and understanding mathematical ideas more elaborately and concretely. With the objective of the ethnomathematics approach, students are expected to be able to construct an understanding of mathematical concepts through their previous experience. To get a deeper grasp of how mathematics relates to other fields of study, to issues in society and the environment, and to how varied users throughout the world effectively use it. the Brazilian educator and mathematician Ubiratan D'Ambrosio coined the term ethnomathematics in 1977 (D'Ambrosio, 1985, 1990, 2001). D'Ambrosio has referred to it as ethnomathematics, or "the mathematics which is practiced among identifiable cultural groups, such as national-tribal societies, labor groups, children of a certain age bracket, professional classes, and so on."

This is in contrast to "academic mathematics," or the mathematics that is taught, practiced, and learned in schools and universities. Ethno-mathematics develops a particular teaching environment for teachers and a customized learning environment for the students. It improves the usability and application of mathematics in actual, realistic circumstances. It expands knowledge of the subject matter being studied and aids in understanding, elucidating, and encouraging reflection on students' and teachers' own thought processes and realities. This may help ethnomathematics build a special method for encouraging students and teachers to think critically.

THREE

LEARNING MATHEMATICS: LOCAL TO GLOBAL PERSPECTIVE

Introduction

Mathematics learning has always been a concern for educators across the globe. The content of mathematics is abstract as compared to other school subjects it eventually becomes a little difficult in terms of its explanation. The nature of mathematics is abstract and symbolic it represents a challenge in front of mathematics teachers to make the content concrete and related to the daily life of the learner's many policies and national curriculum frameworks have advocated that mathematics learning should be done based on problem-solving approach not on the rout learning. To overcome the challenge of teaching mathematics it has also been advocated different policies, that learning mathematics should be considered a process of knowledge-making and **cognitive fun.** The learners should be inclined and link to the philosophy of constructivism, to promote the construction of knowledge by their own.

Learning mathematics suffers from one fundamental issue of its nature i.e. abstractness. As the other school subjects are much more directly related to daily life and more concrete as compared to mathematics, for example, once a teacher is teaching polynomials teacher has to discuss the concept of constants, variables and other related aspects of polynomials. At the same time, the teacher faces the challenge of representing and explaining mathematical concepts like variables and constants in day-to-day life. Therefore, it has been advocated that the content of mathematics should be more concretized and inclined towards the local aspect of learners' surroundings.

Teaching mathematics requires great enthusiasm to make the teaching-learning related to the day-to-day life of the learners. The day-to-day life of the learner means whatever learner is reading in the classroom must relate to and be found in their daily life. So, that they feel connected with the subject and articulate their understanding in a better way which can lead to further interest and good performance in teaching learning of Mathematics.

National Education Policy (NEP) 2020 has also highlighted this aspect of **making the content local**. This means the culture, the environment and the surroundings in which the children are born, should be reflected in the mathematics classrooms and curriculum. The materials that they see around them, let them make visualization of all that in the learning of mathematics. integrate the content of mathematics from their culture, from their society.

As we all know India is a multi-culture society and different cultures have their differences which have a very dipper impact on the understanding and learning system of a child

Learning any content of mathematics has two sides first its structural aspect and second, its functional aspect. Which combination can relate the content of mathematics to day-to-day life and allow the learners to understand the structural and functional part of the content more easily. Therefore, making mathematics local to global should be the vision of mathematics educators, especially school teachers. School teachers are our fundamental building blocks of providing the fundamental concepts of mathematics to our young brains. So, they must understand the utilization and requirement of the cultural aspect of any society and its amalgamation into the teaching-learning of mathematics.

FOUR

MIZO CULTURAL MATERIALS

The present book explains and discusses the various elements of Mizo cultural materials that can be utilized in the teaching-learning of mathematics. The chapters contain the names of all the materials that are included and further elaborated concerning their uses in mathematics teaching and pedagogical articulations. It contains a detailed analysis of a total of 50 indigenous materials concerning their pedagogical analysis suitable for teachers and students for mathematics learning.

FIVE

AIAWT (CRAB TRAP)

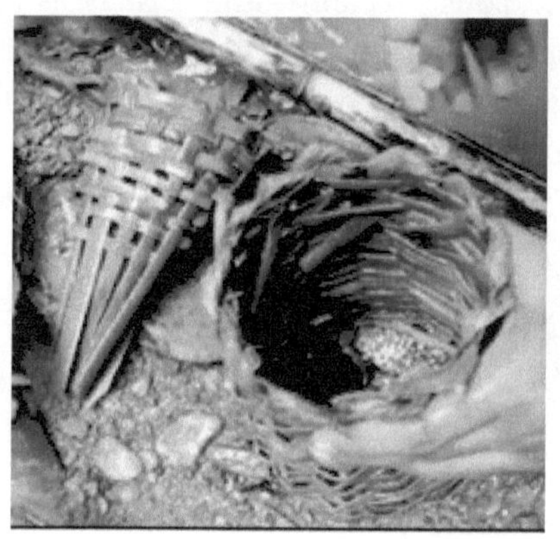

Aiawt

Indigenous Name: Aiawt

About: Aiawt means a bamboo trap for catching small fishes and crabs. The trap consists of an open cylindrical basket. The top of the basket is filled in with a conical funnel made of bamboo slats which are kept wide enough apart by the flow of the water to allow crab and small fishes to enter. Once aside, they cannot escape. The conical funnel is detachable and is removed to allow the fish or crab to be taken out these traps are used in small rivers when the small fishes are swarming.

Mathematical Components: Cylinder, Cone, circle.

Pedagogical Implications: Aiawt is a combination of a cylinder and a cone. It can be used for demonstrating a cone and a cylinder. It can also be used for calculating the volume and surface area of a cylinder.

Application in the Teaching-Learning of Mathematics:

1. Model of a cylinder.
2. Model of a cone.
3. Calculating the volume and surface area of a cylinder.
4. Calculating the volume and surface area of a cone.

SIX

ARBAWM (CHICKEN BASKET)

Arbawm

Indigenous Name: Arbawm

About: Arbawm is a chicken basket made from small split bamboo. This is a home for a hen and chickens. The basket has a square-based and cylindrical body and also has a rectangular opening for in and out. Unlike a regular cylinder shape, it has a hemispherical top which can occupy more space and there used to be a circular opening for carrying the basket.

Mathematical Components: Square, Rectangle, Cylinder.

Pedagogical Implications: It is applicable for explaining squares, rectangles, hemispheres, and cylinders. The material is a combination of an important geometric figure and that explains how important can be in explaining the above-mentioned geometric figures. It can also be used for calculating the volume and surface area of a cylinder and hemisphere.

Application in the Teaching-Learning of Mathematics:

1. Model of a cylinder.
2. Model of a hemisphere.
3. Calculating the volume and surface area of a cylinder.
4. Calculating the volume and surface area of a hemisphere.

SEVEN
BAIBEL (EARTHEN POT)

Baibel (Earthen Pot)

Indigenous Name: Baibel

About: Mizo Bai is a stew cooked from wild edible plants and seasoned with various herbs and spices. The pot that is used for making Bai is called Baibel. The local clay maker used to make it from clay with circular openings and having oval shapes bodies. It was very useful and was available in each and every house in earlier days.

Mathematical Components: Circle, Oval.

Pedagogical Implications: This type of object can be used in teaching a lesson on circles and for explaining oval shapes. The oval shape can be somehow confusing for the learner, especially in lower classes. By showing the above materials, it is believed that the learner can have a clear-cut idea of how an oval looks (visualizing the structural aspects of an oval). Also, it has a circular opening that can be used for explaining a circle and for countering the circumference and area of a circle.

Application in the Teaching-Learning of Mathematics:

1. Model of oval shape.
2. Finding the area and perimeter of a circle.

EIGHT

BELVAL

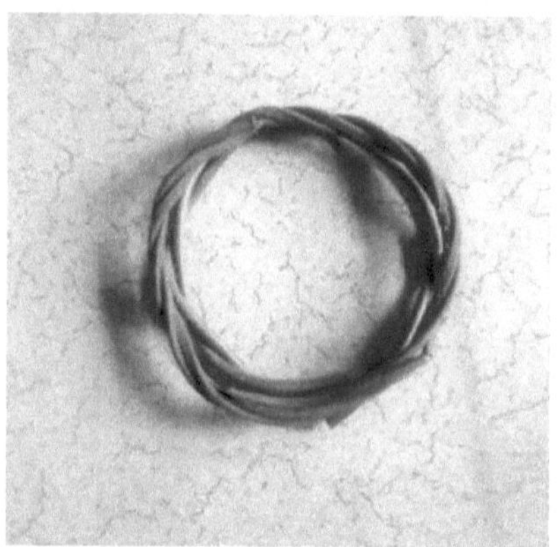

Belval

Indigenous Name: Belval

About: Belval is made from long pieces of creeper from the forest. For making belval, there is no requirement for an artisan and it can simply be made by local people. There was no fixed size for Belval and the size varied based on their needs. It was made in a circular shape and was used for the stand of a traditional Mizo clay pot.

Mathematical Components: Circle.

Pedagogical Implications: It can be used to demonstrate a circle since it has a circular shape and can also be used to counter the volume and surface area of a circle. It can be seen and noted that circular shapes were very useful in earlier days.

Application in the Teaching-Learning of Mathematics:

1. Model of a circle.
2. Calculating the perimeter of a circle.
3. Calculating the area of a circle.

NINE

BERHBU (BRASS BOWL)

Berhbu (Brass Bowl)

Indigenous Name: Berhbu

About: Berhbu is a small bowl made from brass. It was used by Mizo for measuring salt and for holding water for damping cloth when weaving. It was hemispherical in shape with a circular opening.

Mathematical Components: Circle, Hemisphere.

Pedagogical Implications: It can be used for demonstrating circles and hemispheres. Also, it can be used for countering the volume and surface area of a hemisphere. The circular opening can be used to explain the circumference and area of the circle.

Application in the Teaching-Learning of Mathematics:

1. Computing the volume, curved surface area, and whole surface area of the hemisphere.
2. Countering the circumference and area of a circle.
3. Combining the different kinds of geometrical figures and making a meaningful shape.

TEN
BUHTLEI (RICE STIRRER)

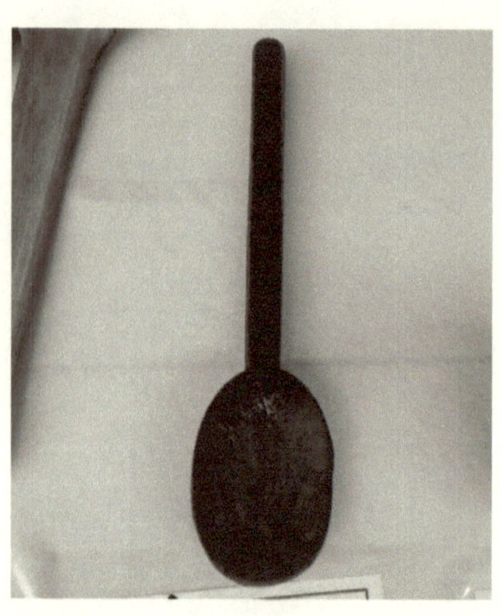

Buhtlei (Rice Stirrer)

Indigenous Name: Buhtlei

About: Rice stirrer is a kitchen material and it is very useful in earlier days. It is made from wood and has a cylindrical handle. The body is made in an oval shape to contain rice. Though, it is a very kitchen material but plays a very important in the kitchen and is used every morning by the time of having breakfast and dinner. It is not only used for stirring rice but sometimes used as a spoon for stirring other cooking vegetables, etc.

Mathematical Components: Cylinder, Curve, Oval.

Pedagogical Implications: It can be used for demonstrating oval shape. It can also be used for calculating the volume and surface area of a triangle.

Application in the Teaching-Learning of Mathematics:

1. Model of an oval.
2. Model of cylinder.
3. Calculating the volume and surface area of a cylinder.

ELEVEN

Chawthlengpui (Mizo Plate/ Common Wooden Plate)

Chawthlengpui

Indigenous Name: Chawthlengpui

About: Chawthlwngpui is a Mizo plate or common wooden plate in the Mizo society of the bygone day. There could never be any distinction between the rich and the poor in meal eating style. They sat together and shared the same food. Generally, thlanvawng (one kind of tree) was used for this plate. It is a circular shape at the top and digs around 1 inch thick from the top so that it can hold rice and other things Also there is a smaller circle for its leg so that it can stand perfectly and there is a space in between by supported from the sides. The size varies by the size of the family.

Mathematical Components: Circle, Frustum.

Pedagogical Implications: It can be used to explain the volume and surface area of a frustum because two circles of different radii can be seen from the top and can be used for explaining the circle.

Application in the Teaching-Learning of Mathematics:

1. Model for frustum.
2. Calculating the volume and surface area of a frustum.
3. Demonstrating circle.

TWELVE
CHEMPUI (DAO)

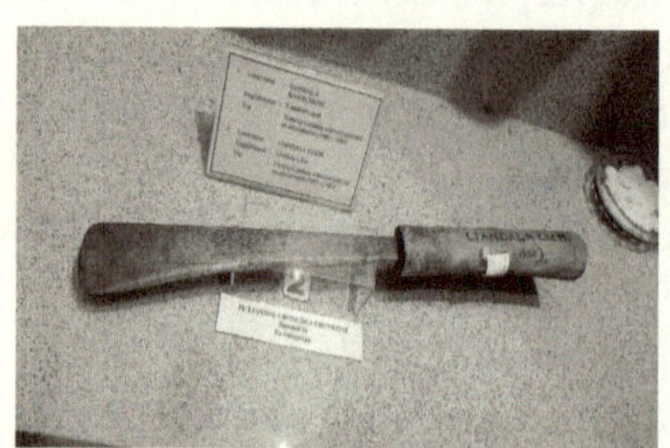

Chempui (Dao)

Indigenous Name: Chempui

About: The most utility materials in the Mizo society. These daos are made in the village forge from iron. The Chempui has a cylindrical handle that supports the sharp iron materials. The handles are made from the root of bamboo in a cylindrical shape. This is used for clearing the jungle, and the broad end is used for sowing the seeds in the ground.

Mathematical Components: Arc of a Circle, Quadrilateral, Cylinder.

Pedagogical Implications: It will be applicable in teaching the arc of a circle, quadrilateral, and cylinder. Though it is not a right circular cylinder it can be imagined as a cylinder.

Application in the Teaching-Learning of Mathematics:

1. Model of a cylinder.
2. Calculating the volume and surface area of a cylinder.

THIRTEEN

CHHEMTHEI

Chhemthei

Indigenous Name: Chhemthei

About: Chhemthei is the most straightforward kitchen material for Mizo and was originally made from bamboo. As time passed later used iron to make it. They made Chhemthei by cutting bamboo between the nodes to form a hollow cylinder for blowing the fire while cooking.

Mathematical Components: Hollow cylinder, circle.

Pedagogical Implications: It can be used in teaching circles and cylinders. It looks simple, but it gives a clear figure of what a cylinder looks like. The hollow cylinder is defined as a cylinder, which is empty from the inside and has some difference between the internal and external radius. The bottom of the hollow cylinder looks like an annular ring. In other words, the bottom of the hollow cylinder resembles a region bounded by two concentric circles.

Application in the Teaching-Learning of Mathematics:

1. It is a model of a hollow cylinder.

FOURTEEN
CHHIHRI (SIEVE)

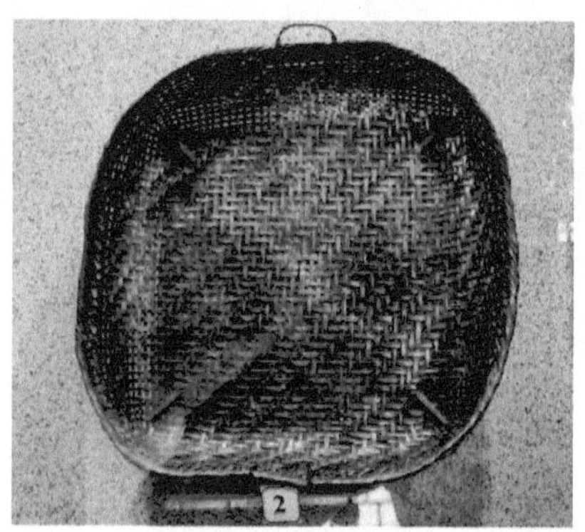

Chhihri (Sieve)

Indigenous Name: Sieve

About: Chhihri is a filtering tray, made of bamboo. It has a square base and opening but the height varies forming a cuboidal shape. It was useful for filtering and cleaning different eatable things especially while cooking. This Chhihri can be found in every household. Its sole purpose is to filter out rice from chaff.

Mathematical Components: Square, Cuboid, Rectangle.

Pedagogical Implications: A sieve is a model of a square and cuboid. It can be used for demonstrating a square and a cuboid. It can also be used for calculating the volume and surface area of a cuboid. It can also be applicable for computing the area and perimeter of a square/rectangle.

Application in the Teaching-Learning of Mathematics:

1. Model of a square/rectangle.
2. Calculating the area and perimeter of a square/rectangle.
3. Model of a cuboid.
4. Computing the capacity and surface area of a cuboid.

FIFTEEN

DARKHUANG/ ZAMLUANG (MUSICAL DRUM)

Darkhuang/Zamluang

Indigenous Name: Darkhuang/Zamluang

About: Darkhuang, also known as Zamluang (Jamluang), is a large musical drum made from brass and used as part of cultural activities of dance and festival revelry in the State of Mizoram in the northeastern part of India. It is a costly drum. The beating of this dar or drum or gong is known in the local Mizo language as "Darkhuang-Tum". In ancient days it was an important musical instrument used to convey or exchange messages.

Mathematical components: Hemisphere, Hallow Cylinder.

Pedagogical Implications: It is applicable for explaining hemispheres, and cylinders. The material is made of a combination of an important geometric figure and that explains how important can be in explaining the above-mentioned geometric figures. It can be used for calculating the volume and surface area of a hemisphere. It can also be used for calculating the circumference and area of a circle.

Application in the Teaching-Learning of Mathematics:

1. Model of a cylinder.
2. Model of a hemisphere.
3. Calculating the volume and surface area of a cylinder.
4. Calculating the volume and surface area of a hemisphere

SIXTEEN

DARNGUN KUAL (SPIRAL BRASS BANGLES)

Darngun Kual

Indigenous Name: Darngun Kual
About: Darngun Kual is a Mizo traditional brass bangle and is usually worn by women of well-to-do families. It is circular in shape and is made from brass.

Mathematical Components: Circle.

Pedagogical Implications: It can be used for demonstrating a circle. Since it is circular in shape, it can also be used for computing the area and circumference of a circle.

Application in the Teaching-Learning of Mathematics:

1. Model of a circle.
2. Calculating the area of a circle.
3. Calculating the circumference of a circle.

SEVENTEEN

Fairel Bel (An Earthen Vessel or Cleaned Rice Vessel)

Fairel Bel

Indigenous Name: Fairel Bel

About: Fairel Bel is the material where clean rice is kept ready for cooking and this belongs to the kitchen household. It is made from bamboo that has a square base a circular opening and a conical shape cover that protects rice from dust particles, insects, and rats. It is developed by weaving the thin bamboo sheets (stripes) together in a crisscross way together. It has four small bamboo bases (stand) as a support and balance to a square base.

Mathematical Components: Square, Circle, and Cone.

Pedagogical Implications: It can be used in demonstrating circles, squares, and cones. Also, the learner might be able to counter the volume and surface area.

It is relevant in the present-day mathematics content that the learner might know and understand the beauty of mathematical figures and how cones, circles, and squares must be related.

Application in the Teaching-Learning of Mathematics:

1. Calculating the capacity, and lateral surface area of a cone.
2. Identifying and computing circles, square, and their related aspects.
3. Arranging the different kinds of geometrical figures and making a meaningful shape.

EIGHTEEN
FAVAH (SICKLE)

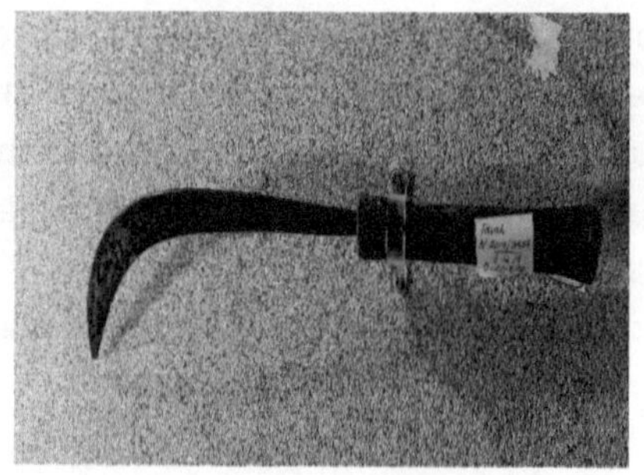

Favah (Sickle)

Indigenous Name: Favah

About: A sickle is a Mizo farming tool having a curved blade and a bamboo handle. It's meant to be used with one hand, typically to harvest bundles of plants (like grasses or grains) by cutting them at the base. It is also used in the paddy field for cutting rice.

Mathematical Components: Curve, Cylinder.

Pedagogical Implications: Favah can be used for demonstrating cylinders and curves. Bamboo handles can be used for calculating the volume and surface of a cylinder. The metal can also be used to explain the curve.

Application in the Teaching-Learning of Mathematics:

1. Model of a cylinder
2. Model of a curve.
3. Calculating the volume and surface area of a cylinder.

NINETEEN

FENTHLIR (LADLE/ DIPPER)

Fenthlir (Ladle/Dipper)

Indigenous Name: Fenthlir

About: Fenthlir (Ladle/Dipper) is a Mizo traditional mug with a long handle that was very useful in earlier days. It is made from a gourd which is used for drawing water from the natural water holes. It has a hemispherical body and a cylindrical handle with a conical shape at the end. The gourd is initially dried and cleaned from the inside to prepare a hollow mug and then it is cut in a hemispherical shape along with a cylindrical handle.

Mathematical Components: Hemisphere, Circle, Cylinder.

Pedagogical Implications: This material can be used for demonstrating hemispherical shapes and explaining the related mathematical aspects. Fenthlir is a local product, so students in a mathematics classroom can easily relate to their daily lives.

Application in the Teaching-Learning of Mathematics:

1. Calculating the surface area of a hemisphere.
2. Calculating the volume of a hemisphere
3. Measuring the radius and diameter of a hemisphere
4. Demonstrating hemisphere.

TWENTY

FUNGKI (GUN POWDER CONTAINER)

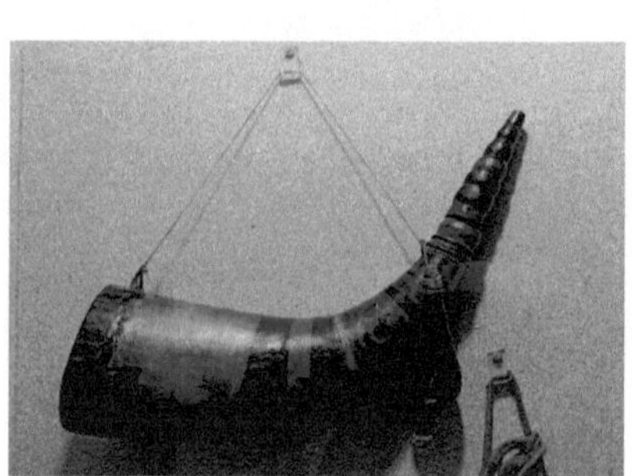

Fungki (Gun Powder Container)

Indigenous Name: Fungki

About: It is a gun-powder container made of a bison horn with a stopper using a carving technique. The surface is painted in red and black color. The gunpowder container was used for keeping gunpowder by the time of hunting animals.

Mathematical Components: Cone.

Pedagogical Implications: It is an application for teaching and learning conical and circular shape objects. The conical-look materials can help the learner understand the shape of a cone and a circle. It can be used for calculating the volume and surface area of a cone and countering the perimeter and area of a circle.

Application in the Teaching-Learning of Mathematics:

1. Calculate the volume and the surface area of the cone.
2. Computing the area and perimeter of a circle.

TWENTY-ONE
HACHHEK (ADZE)

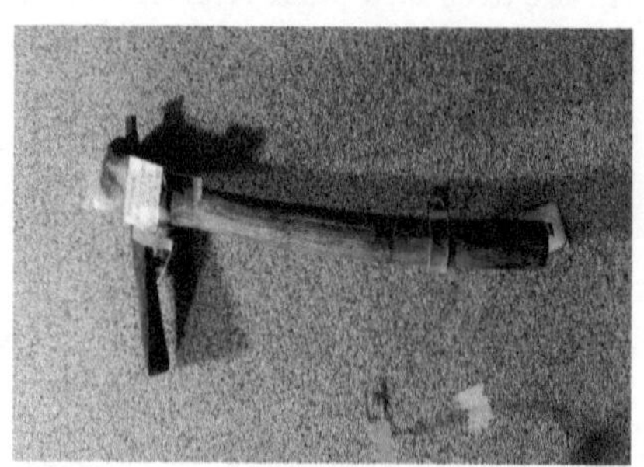

Hachhek (Adze)

Indigenous Name: Hachhek

About: Adze was a Mizo traditional tool used by woodworkers for cutting and trimming rough wooden planks, shaping and smoothing wooden surfaces, and splitting and opening out bamboo. It has a triangular head with a long bamboo handle.

Mathematical Components: Cylinder, Curve, Triangle.

Pedagogical Implications: Adze can be used for explaining cylinders, curves, and triangles. The bamboo handle is cylindrical and can be used for calculating the volume and surface of a cylinder. The head can also be used for explaining triangles and a curve.

Application in the Teaching-Learning of Mathematics:

1. Model of a cylinder
2. Model of triangle and curve.
3. Calculating the volume and surface area of a cylinder.

TWENTY-TWO
Hmui (A Spinning Wheel)

Hmui (A Spinning Wheel)

Indigenous name: Hmui

About: Hmui or the spinning wheel is made from wood and bamboo cane, the actual spindle being made of iron. The stand of the wheel is also made of wood. It was used for extracting the thread. It is used scientifically to create thread from rolled cotton

Mathematical Components: Triangle, Hexagon, 600, perpendicular, quarter circle.

Pedagogical Implications: A Spinning Wheel can be used for demonstrating triangles, hexagons, and 600. It can also be used for calculating the area of a triangle.

Application in the Teaching-Learning of Mathematics:

1. Model of a hexagon.
2. Model of a triangle.
3. Calculating the area of a triangle.
4. Counting the triangles.

TWENTY-THREE
HNAM

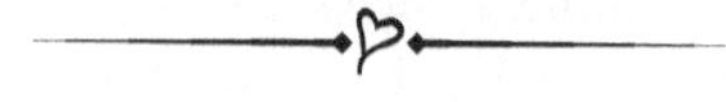

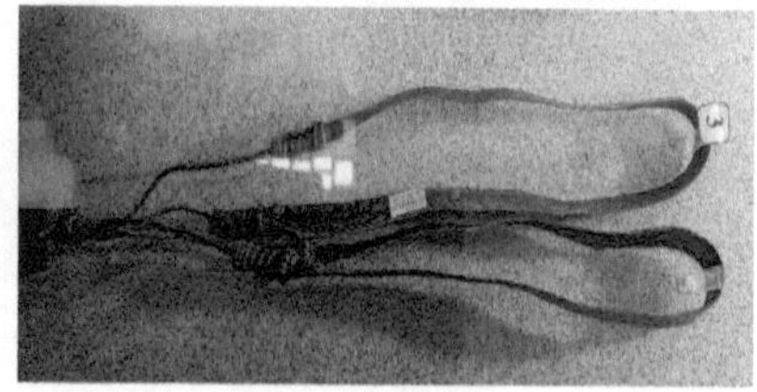

Hnam

Indigenous Name: Hnam

About: A basket strap is a Mizo traditional material used for carrying different kinds of baskets. It was made from bamboo stripes by the local artisan. It is rectangular in shape and very long and can form a curve as well. The flat part was for the headrest and was joined with bamboo rope.

Mathematical Components: Rectangle, curve.

Pedagogical Implications: A basket strap can be used for demonstrating a rectangle and a curve. It can help the learner understand a rectangle. It can also be used for computing the area and perimeter of a rectangle. The strap is very flexible and it can form a beautiful parabolic curve, circle, etc.

Application in the Teaching-Learning of Mathematics:

1. Model of a rectangle.
2. Calculating the area of a rectangle.
3. Calculating the perimeter of a rectangle.

TWENTY-FOUR

Hnawhtawt (A Trap for Killing Rat)

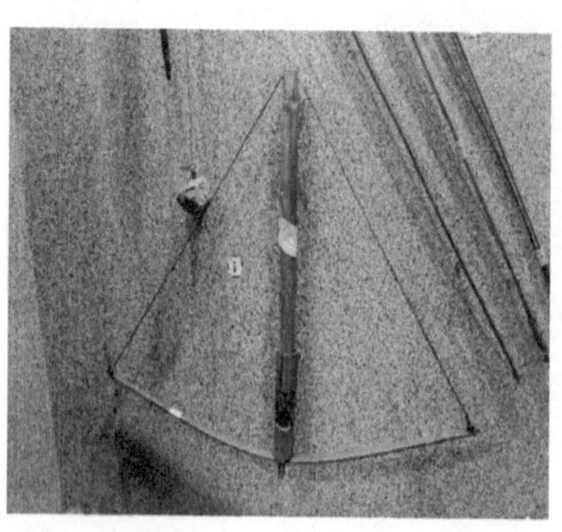

Hnawhtawt (A Trap for Killing Rat)

Indigenous Name: Hnawhtawt

About: Hnawhtawt is a trap for killing rats. It was very useful in earlier days. It was made from bamboo. A strong lever was attached at the end of a hollow cylinder and was connected with a string that looked like a similar triangle. There was a circular opening for keeping the bait. A small hole was made and a little string that worked as a trigger passed through the hole. By the time of eating the bait, the rats used to bite that string and that's pulled the trigger.

Mathematical Components: Hallow Cylinder, Circle, Similar Triangle.

Pedagogical Implications: Hnawhtawt is applicable for demonstrating a hollow cylinder, circle, and a similar triangle. It can be used for computing the area and circumference of a triangle. It can also be used for calculating the surface area of a hollow cylinder.

Application in the Teaching-Learning of Mathematics:
1. Model of a circle.
2. Models of a hollow cylinder.
3. Calculating the area and circumference of a circle.

TWENTY-FIVE
HREIPUI (AXE)

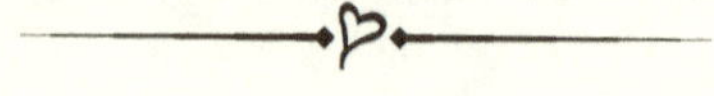

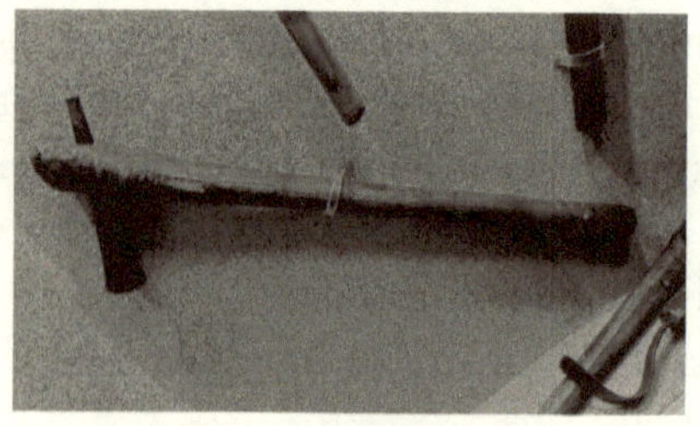

Hreipui (Axe)

Indigenous Name: Hreipui

About: Hreipui is a traditional axe found in a Mizo society used for cutting firewood in small pieces in rural areas. It contains bamboo as a handle in which an iron head is inserted in such a way that it can be used for cutting and smoothing the wooden surface.

Mathematical Components: Cylinder, Curve, Triangle.

Pedagogical Implications: Axe can be used for explaining cylinders, curves, and triangles. The bamboo handle is cylindrical and can be used for calculating the volume and surface of a cylinder. The head can also be used for explaining triangles and a curve.

Application in the Teaching-Learning of Mathematics:

1. Model of a cylinder
2. Model of triangle and curve.
3. Calculating the volume and surface area of a cylinder.

TWENTY-SIX

IPTE PUI (MIZO TRADITIONAL BAG)

Ipte Pui (Mizo Traditional Bag)

Indigenous Name: Ipte Pui

About: Ipte pui was made from available cloth. There are no perfect or actual sizes for the Mizo traditional bag. The size is varied depending upon the needs of the family or per person. It was a local made in a cuboidal shape having a strong strap that will hold heavy things. It was usually used for carrying dao, food, water bottles, etc. by the time of working.

Mathematical Components: Cuboid, curve.

Pedagogical Implications: The Mizo traditional bag can be used for explaining cuboids and curves. It can also be used for calculating the volume and surface area of a cuboid. The strap can also form a parabolic curve.

Application in the Teaching-Learning of Mathematics:

1. Model of a cuboid
2. Calculating the volume and surface area of a cuboid.

TWENTY-SEVEN

KAHPUK (MIZO BAMBOO TOY GUN)

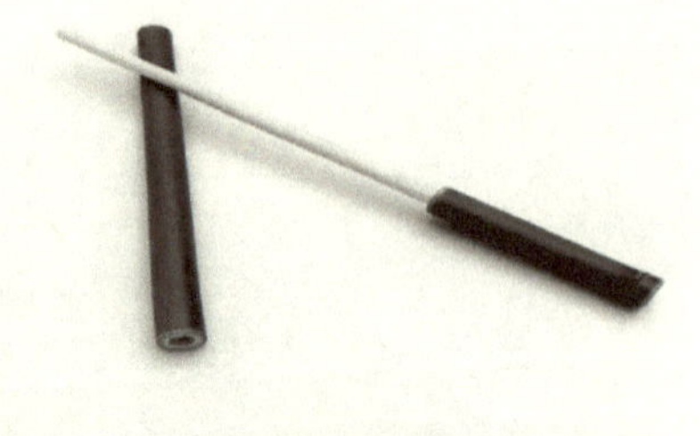

Kahpuk

Indigenous name: Kahpuk

About: Kahpuk is a Mizo Bamboo toy gun made from a small bamboo. It is made by the elders for the children. It has a hollow cylindrical barrel and a handle that usually used to be the size of a barrel. It also had a cylindrical stick with the size of a hollow cylinder but shorter than the barrel. For firing the bullet, the handle is pressed and it is fired. With this, children used to play and enjoy their childhood. Children in rural areas are still enjoying Kahpuk.

Mathematical Components: Hallow Cylinder, Circle, Cylinder

Pedagogical Implications: The material is made up of a combination of a cylindrical family and can be used for demonstrating a hollow cylinder and a cylinder. It can also be used for calculating the volume and surface area of a cylinder.

Application in the Teaching-Learning of Mathematics:

1. Model of a cylinder.
2. Model of a hollow cylinder.
3. Calculating the volume and surface area of a cylinder.

TWENTY-EIGHT
KAIHBU (LATTU)

Kaihbu (Lattu)

Indigenous Name: Kaihbu

About: Lattu or spinning tops are used to play games in Mizoram. This has been a traditional game of Mizo which used to be liked and played by every kid, but now it is losing its importance and enjoyment due to the availability of the internet but still enjoyed in rural areas. It was made from wood in a conical shape and hemispherical top for balance.

Mathematical Components: Cone.

Pedagogical Implications: It has a shape of inverted conical shape and circular opening at the top that can be used for demonstrating cone and circle. It can also be used for countering the volume and surface area of a cone. Perimeter and area of circle can be calculated using this material.

Application in the Teaching-Learning of Mathematics:

1. Model of a cone
2. Calculating the area and volume of a cone.

TWENTY-NINE
KALCHHET (STILT)

Kalchhet (Stilt)

Indigenous Name: Kalchhet

About: Walking on stilts is one of the Mizo games. The stilt is made from bamboo. These bamboo sticks are specially design in such a way that a small portion of the foot can be placed over that and remaining part is used as a tall handle for maintaining the coordination and balance of the player. This handle and the standing paddle are made of a single bamboo so that it can be enough strong to handle the weight of a person. With the help of this, children and adults used to play the games in which they stand on this bamboo and used to walk or run with the help of stilt.

Mathematical Components: Hallow Cylinder and Cylindrical structure.

Pedagogical Implications: The material is made up of a bamboo which is sharpen at the top for making handle and adjusted as a paddle for putting foot. It can be generally utilised for explaining cylinder and straight lines as well as concept of symmetry (as it works in a pair for two legs) both are symmetrical geometrically. It can also be used for demonstrating a hollow cylinder and can be used for demonstrating and calculating the volume and surface area of a cylinder.

Application in the Teaching-Learning of Mathematics:

1. Model of a cylinder.
2. Calculating the volume and surface area of a cylinder.

THIRTY
Kʜᴏ /Fᴀᴡɴɢ

Kho /Fawng

Indigenous Name: Kho/Fawng

About: It is a Mizo basket used for measuring rice and used for keeping clean rice ready for cooking. Also, it can be used for keeping vegetables. Thin strips of bamboo are used to make this basket and require a skilled artisan. It has a square base, a cylindrical body, and a circular opening. Small baskets and very common and useful and were available in every house in earlier days.

Mathematical Components: Square, circle, and cylinder.

Pedagogical Implications: By seeing the object, it can be seen how geometrical shapes can produce such a beautiful and useful material by mixing the shapes. It can be used for teaching and learning mathematical components such as squares, circles, and cylinders. It can also be used for finding the circumference and area of a circle.

Application in the Teaching-Learning of Mathematics:

1. Model of a square
2. Computing the area and circumference of a circle.
3. Calculating the volume of a circle.

THIRTY-ONE

KHUANGPUI (A COMMON LARGE DRUM)

Khuangpui

Indigenous Name: Khuangpui

About: Khuangpui is a Mizo traditional drum and is available in each and every church in Mizoram. It is made from wood and cowhide. The cylindrical drum was hollow having a circular opening that was covered by cowhide and could produce sound by beating the drum.

Mathematical Components: Hallow Cylinder, Circle.

Pedagogical Implications: Khuangpui is a hollow cylinder and can be used for demonstrating a hollow cylinder. It can also be used for computing the lateral surface area of a cylinder.

Application in the Teaching-Learning of Mathematics:

1. Model of a cylinder.
2. Calculating the curved surface area of a cylinder.

THIRTY-TWO

Khuhhriang (Mizo Traditional Bowl)

Khuhhriang

Indigenous Name: Khuhhriang

About: Khuhhriang (mizo traditional bowl) is a traditional material of the Mizo culture used for keeping eatable materials. Earlier it was made of clay and in recent days it was made from aluminium by a local artisan. It was a kitchen material and mainly used for serving vegetables while dining. It was very useful in the early days. It has a circular open and hemispherical body to contain some vegetables with soup. Also, it has a small circular support as a stand which combinedly attains the beautiful shapes of a bowl which is slightly flattered in shape.

Mathematical Components: Circle, Hemisphere.

Pedagogical Implications: It can be used for demonstrating circles and hemispheres. Also, it can be used for countering the volume and surface area of a hemisphere. The circular opening can be used to explain the circumference and area of the circle.

Application in the Teaching-Learning of Mathematics:

1. Computing the volume, curved surface area, and whole surface area of the hemisphere.
2. Countering the circumference and area of a circle.
3. Combining the different kinds of geometrical figures and making a meaningful shape.

THIRTY-THREE

Mau Haileng No (Ordinary Bamboo Cup)

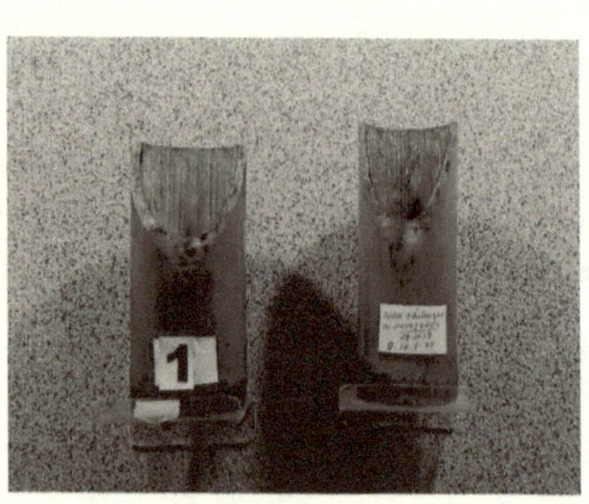

Mau Haileng No

Indigenous Name: Mau Haileng No
About: Mau Haileng No is a Mizo traditional cup usually used for drinking Mizo traditional beer. It was made from

bamboo and the bamboo was cut before the nodes forming a cylinder. The other end has a diagonal cut semi-circular opening for easy pouring. The size can vary depending upon the requirement and there were no fixed sizes.

Mathematical Components: Cylinder, diagonally cut semi-circular shape.

Pedagogical Implications: It is applicable for demonstrating a cylinder. Also, the learner can easily understand the surface area of a cylinder just by seeing that object and can also counter the volume or capacity of a cylinder. It is very relevant in the present-day mathematics curriculum that by knowing the shape of the cylinder, the learner can separate the object easily. Also, there are many cylinder-shaped objects in modern days, and with the concept's knowledge, it will be easy to understand.

Application in the Teaching-Learning of Mathematics:

1. Model of a cylinder.
2. Calculating the volume and surface area of a cylinder.

THIRTY-FOUR

Mizo In (Typical Mizo House)

Mizo In

Indigenous Name: Mizo In

About: The houses built by the Lushai tribe of Mizoram, predominantly use bamboo and wood in their construction. Most of the houses are built on the slopes and are invariably supported by wooden posts of varied lengths so that the house is balanced horizontally with the level of the road. The rectangular doors and windows are usually of bamboo matting and these are fastened against the wall. It may be noted that in some cases the floor, doors, and windows are made of wooden planks, while in others split bamboos are used instead. The body of the hose is a cuboidal shape and a triangular shape at the top.

Mathematical Components: Rectangle, Cuboid, And Triangle.

Pedagogical Implications: It will be applicable in a cuboid, rectangle, and triangle. It is relevant in the mathematics aspects like calculating the curved surface area and volume of a cuboid. It can also be used for computing the area of a rectangle and a triangle.

Application in the Teaching-Learning of Mathematics:

1. Computing the area of a rectangle and a square.
2. Calculating the volume and surface area of a cuboid.

THIRTY-FIVE

NGHAWNGKAWL (YOKE)

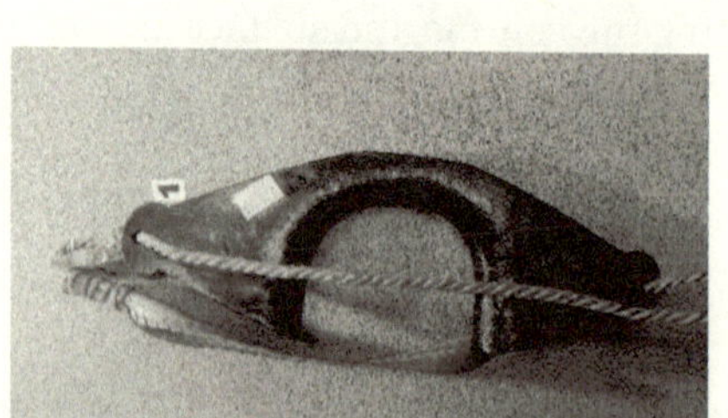

Nghawngkawl

Indigenous Name: Nghawngkawl

About: It is a curved shaped material made of wood generally used for carrying heavy baskets. It is a kind of neck and shoulder support to hang the basket and carry it on the hilly areas. It is generally local made product, very famous in the tribal culture.

Mathematical Components: Semicircle, curve.

Pedagogical Implications: This kind of material can be used for explaining unusual geometrical shapes as well as semicircles and curves.

Application in the Teaching-Learning of Mathematics:

1. Model of a semicircle.
2. Unusual mathematical curves and geometrical shapes.

THIRTY-SIX
PAIKAWNG (OPEN WEAVE CARRYING BASKET)

Paikawng

Indigenous Name: Paikawng
About: The paikawng is an open weave carrying basket made and used by the Mizo tribe of Mizoram. This basket

is generally used by women as a rough work basket for carrying firewood, bamboo water tubes, etc. The basket made entirely of bamboo outer splits, is carried over the back with a strap resting on the head. The basket has an extremely strong combination which is very resistant to vertical loads. This is due to the construction pattern as well as the fact that fairly thick strips of bamboo are used. The Paikawng has a square base and transforms into a circle at the rim. To the craftsmen making this basket, the height may vary depending upon the need and the user.

Mathematical Components: Circle, Square, Straight lines, symmetry, counting, arranging the sticks (bamboo sticks), frustum, sections of frustum.

Pedagogical Implications: This material can be used for demonstrating Circle, Square, Straight lines, symmetry, counting, arranging the sticks (bamboo sticks), frustum, and sections of frustum. As well as demonstration of the frustum and its related aspects like the area of a frustum, radius, and diameter of a rim can be done. Calculation of volume and surface area can also be done.

Application in the Teaching-Learning of Mathematics:

1. Model of a frustum.
2. Calculating the volume and surface area of a frustum.
3. Finding the area of a square and circle.

THIRTY-SEVEN
PHENGLAWNG (MIZO BAMBOO FLUTE)

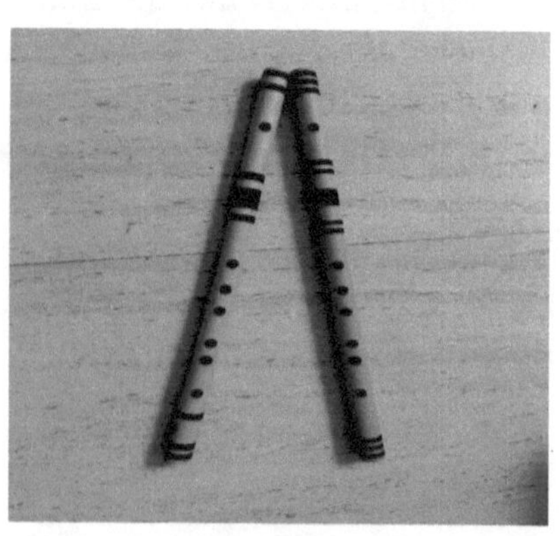

Phenglawng

Indigenous name: Phenglawng

About: Phenglawng is a traditional Mizo bamboo flute. It is made from a small bamboo cutting before the nodes forming a hollow cylinder. Originally, Phenglawng had only three circular holes producing three different sounds.

Mathematical Components: Hollow Cylinder, Circle.

Pedagogical Implications: The Bamboo Flute is applicable for teaching a hollow cylinder and a circle since it has a circular opening. It can be used for computing the surface area of a hollow cylinder. It can also be used for calculating the circumference and area of a circle.

Application in the Teaching-Learning of Mathematics:

1. Model of a hollow cylinder.
2. Calculating the surface area of a hollow cylinder.
3. Calculating the circumference and area of a circle.

THIRTY-EIGHT

Raw Chaicheh (A Bamboo Tong)

Raw Chaicheh (A Bamboo Tong)

Indigenous Name: Raw Chaicheh

About: Raw Chaicheh is a material used in the kitchen for holding and grabbing equipment, it is made in a very traditional style made up of bamboo. It consists of two straight bamboos around one and a half feet long. It is also used for moving hot cooking pots and for taking charcoal out of the burning fire in the early times.

Mathematical Components: Straight Line, Angles (can be placed at different angles), Semi-oval.

Pedagogical Implications: It is very much relevant in the present day's geometry that with the help of that object, the learners can have a clear understanding and the importance of straight lines and different angles can be demonstrated from it.

Teaching straight lines and angles since it is movable it can make different angles like 30, 45o, 60o, 90o. Etc. and can be used to demonstrate and measure the different angles in the classrooms. It can also be used for showing and visualizing the intersection of two lines and the formation of angles by them. The Chaicheh can be useful in teaching geometry to elementary students.

Application in the Teaching-Learning of Mathematics:

1. Demonstration and measurement of angles
2. Showing the intersection of the two straight lines

THIRTY-NINE

Sahdal Thang (A Snare for Terrestrial Birds)

Sahdal Thang

Indigenous Name: Sahdal Thang

About: Sahdal Thang is one of the most popular snares for Mizo. It was made from small and thin strips of bamboo converted as a rope. It can also be seen from the picture how the snare works. It had a curvy lever to support the circular shape snare and a straight lock at the bottom and that was a trigger as well. As soon as the birds crossed the path touching the trigger, the bird was caught.

Mathematical Components: Circle, Straight Line, Curve.

Pedagogical Implications: It can be used to demonstrate a circle, straight line, and curve. The angle of the curve is very flexible and can produce different parabolic curves depending upon the choice. It can also be used for calculating the area and perimeter of a circle.

Application in the Teaching-Learning of Mathematics:

1. Model of a circle.
2. Calculating the area of a circle.
3. Calculating the circumference of a circle.

FORTY
SAIHLUM

Saihlum

Indigenous Name: Saihlum

About: Saihlum(pellet) was usually made and used by children from clay in a spherical shape. The process of making pellets is by taking clay from the forest where the clay was softer and smoothy (Sawntlung lei*) for making spherical-shaped pellets. The clay was then mixed with water to prepare pellets. After that, they roll in a spherical shape and dry by putting under the sun or by heating in a fireplace. After it dries it becomes ready to be used, mainly these pellets are used for hunting birds.

Mathematical Components: Sphere, volume, and surface area of a sphere.

Pedagogical Implications: It can be used for teaching a sphere since it is a completely spherical object and very simple and easy to understand. There are countless hollow and non-hollow spherical materials in the present day and can be considered that it is very relevant in present days. Without a spherical shape, it is incomplete.

Application in the Teaching-Learning of Mathematics:

1. Perfect model of a sphere.
2. Calculating the volume and surface area of a sphere.

* It's a Mizo word which means smooth clay.

FORTY-ONE

SAMKHUIH (MIZO TRADITIONAL COMB)

Samkhuih

Indigenous Name: Samkuih

About: Samkhuih is a Mizo traditional come and is made from bamboo. In earlier days, women were not the only ones who kept their hair long, even men were keeping their hair long enough for using the comb which was useful for both. Also, they used to comb their hair in the morning by exposing it to the sun, especially in winter. The process of making a traditional comb was that bamboo was cut nearly the size of a toothpick in a cylindrical structure with a conical shape spike that was tied in the straight-line frame leaving a space for holding.

Mathematical Components: Straight Line, Cone, Triangle, Cylinder.

Pedagogical Implications: It can be a good example of showing how small geometric objects can play an important role like the small cone in this comb mixing with a small cylinder. Though they are very small still they did not lose their property. Also, there is a straight line and a triangular top at the end.

Application in the Teaching-Learning of Mathematics:

1. Explaining straight-line
2. Applicable for counting.
3. Associate the different kinds of geometrical figures and make a meaningful shape.

FORTY-TWO

Sa-Um Bur (Fermented Pig Fats Jar)

Sa-Um Bur

Indigenous Name: Sa-Um Bur

About: Sa-um bur is made from a bottled gourd. The process of making sa-um is that Fats of pigs are mainly collected from the inner abdominal portion (sometimes fats from other parts of the pig's body were also used), cooked and torn/chopped into pieces, and placed in a special container called "Sa-Um Bur". It is an important component in Mizo society and is been used till the present day. It has a circular open so that it can easily be taken out and has a spherical body.

Mathematical Components: Circle, Sphere.

Pedagogical Implications: It has a circular opening with a short neck and a spherical body. It will be applicable in a teaching circle and sphere. It is relevant in the mathematics aspects like calculating the curved surface area and volume. This material can be useful for demonstrating the different aspects of a sphere. It represents the three-dimensional shape and can be treated as a working model.

Application in the Teaching-Learning of Mathematics:

1. Combination of sphere and circle.
2. Calculation of curved surface area and volume.
3. Representation of curved surface area and volume.

FORTY-THREE

SEKI NO(MITHUN HORN DRINKING VESSEL)

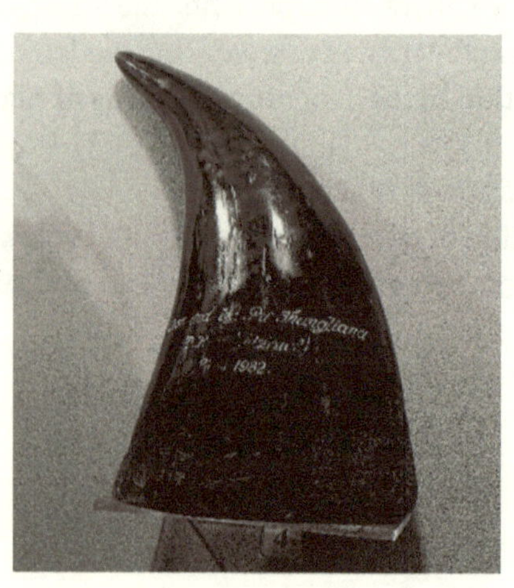

Seki No

Indigenous Name: Seki No

About: Seki no (Mithun horn drinking vessel) is a traditional Mizo rice beer cup used for drinking different kinds of Mizo traditional beer. Mithun (Bos frontalis), a magnificent semi-domesticated and unique bovine species, is believed to have originated more than 8000 years ago. Mithun is a valued animal in the life of the tribal people of Mizoram. The Mithun horn is a conical shape structure material and was very useful in earlier days.

Mathematical Components: Circle, Cone, volume, and surface area of a cone.

Pedagogical Implications: It is an application for teaching and learning conical and circular shape objects. The conical-look materials can help the learner understand the shape of a cone and a circle. It can be used for calculating the volume and surface area of a cone and countering the perimeter and area of a circle.

Application in the Teaching-Learning of Mathematics:

1. Calculate the volume and the surface area of the cone.
2. Computing the area and perimeter of a circle.

FORTY-FOUR
SUK (PESTLE)

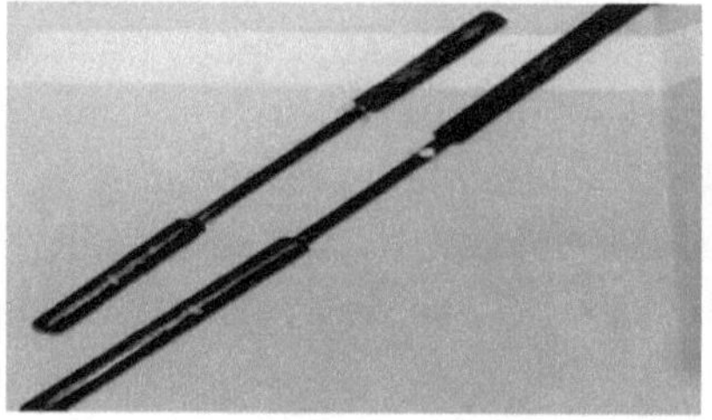

Suk

Indigenous Name: Suk

About: The pestle was made from strong wood in a cylindrical shape having a smaller cylindrical handle with a hemispherical end. In earlier days, harvesting or jhum cultivation or having paddy fields were the main earning for a living and it was practiced by every family, though they did not have a plain area for paddy, they used to plant in the mountainside. After all the hard work was done, the pestle was needed and played an important role in those days. It is mainly used for cleaning the husk by putting the rice in the mortar and by grinding with a pestle.

Mathematical Components: Cylinder, Hemisphere.

Pedagogical Implications: It can be used for demonstrating a cylinder and a hemisphere since it has a cylindrical and hemispherical shape. It can also be used for calculating the volume and surface area of cylindrical and hemispheres. Also, it is a perfect combination of two geometrical shapes that form a relevant and beautiful shape.

Application in the Teaching-Learning of Mathematics:

1. Model of cylinder.
2. Model of hemisphere.
3. Perfect combination of cylinder and hemisphere.

FORTY-FIVE
SUM (MORTAR)

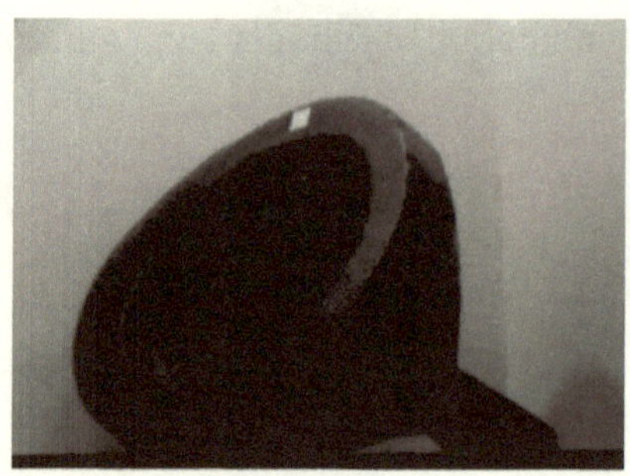

Sum

Indigenous Name: Sum

About: Mizo traditional mortar is made from a big and strong wood. The first process was taking a big log from the forest and cutting it into a cylindrical shape. After that, the body was designed into an inverted conical shape having a cylindrical stand with a conical spike. The purpose of the spike is for a smooth landing and a kind of lock since they used to dig the mud for placing the motor to avoid shaking and moving while working to remove the husk.

Mathematical Components: Inverted Cone, Circle.

Pedagogical Implications: It has a shape of inverted conical shape and a circular opening at the top that can be used for demonstrating cones and circles. It can also be used for countering the volume and surface area of a cone. The perimeter and area of the circle can be calculated using this material.

Application in the Teaching-Learning of Mathematics:

1. Model of a cone.
2. Calculating the volume of a cone.
3. Calculating curved surface area and total surface area of a cone.
4. Area and Circumference of a circle.

FORTY-SIX

Suvel (Cotton Winding Machine)

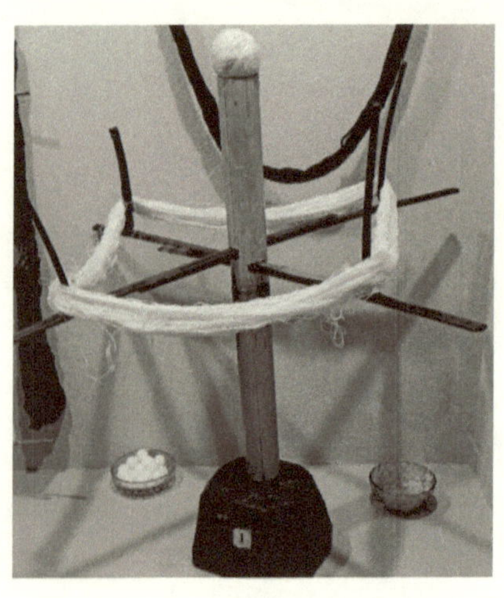

Suvel

Indigenous Name: Suvel

About: Suvel is a revolving tool with four extendable arms around which a skein of cotton yarn is put to make the yarn into a ball. There may be two or three kinds of suvel. It is made from wood and bamboo. It has a cylindrical post and a wooden stand as a base. Four holes are made in a cylindrical post to put the straight arms perpendicular to each other forming a vertically opposite angle.

Mathematical Components: Cylinder, Perpendicular, Straight Line, and Vertically Opposite Angle (V.O.A)

Pedagogical Implications: Suvel contains different mathematical shapes and structures and can be used for demonstrating Cylinder, Perpendicular, Straight Line, and Vertically Opposite Angle (V.O.A). It can also be used for calculating the volume and lateral surface area of a cylinder. Since the arms intersect each other, the right angle and vertically opposite angle can be seen.

Application in the Teaching-Learning of Mathematics:

1. Model of a cylinder.
2. Calculating the volume and surface area of a cylinder.
3. Contain 90^0, perpendicular, and vertically opposite angle.

FORTY-SEVEN
TAWTAWRAWT

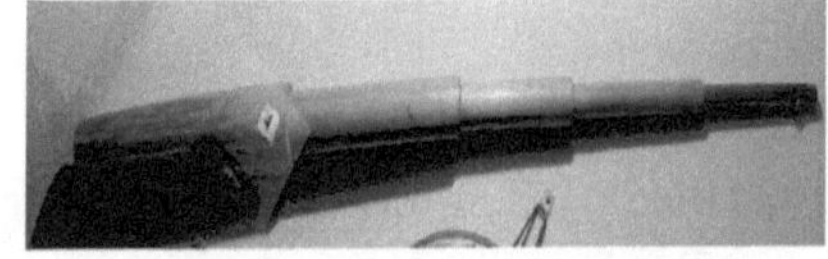

Tawtawrawt

Indigenous Name: Tawtawrawt

About: This is a bamboo trumpet. A number of bamboo hollow cylindrical tubes are cut off. The bigger tubes are joined by inserting them into the smaller tubes. Many bamboo tubes are joined one after another till the last tube happens to be the size of a forefinger from where the trumpet is to be blown. A dry empty gourd, the bottom part being cut off is joined with the bigger end of the bamboo tube. The whole length can be more than five feet. It is usually blown in the jhum to tell their whereabouts and presence and also to pass the time and relieve their loneliness.

Mathematical Components: Hallow Cylinder, Circle.

Pedagogical Implications: The bamboo trumpet is a cylindrical material. It can be used to demonstrate a hollow cylinder. It can be used for calculating the lateral surface area of a circle. It can be seen from the material that how geometrical shapes can be of such importance from earlier till today.

Application in the Teaching-Learning of Mathematics:

1. Model of a hollow cylinder.
2. Calculating the surface area of a hollow cylinder.

FORTY-EIGHT
THLANGRA

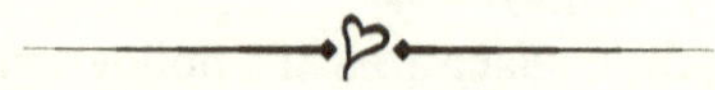

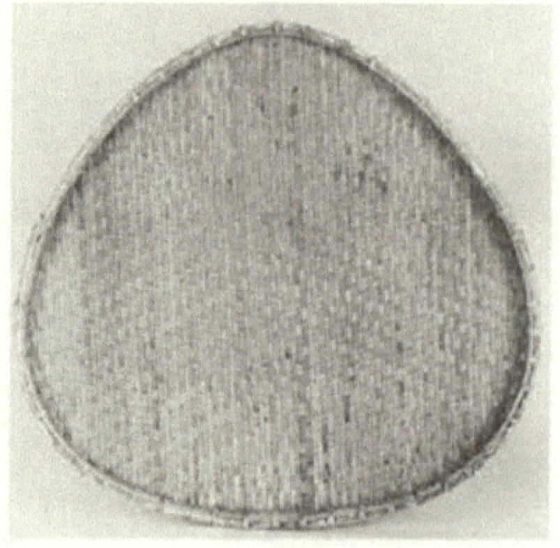

Thlangra

Indigenous Name: Thlangra

About: The thlangra is a winnowing tray used by the Lushai tribe of Mizoram. The triangular thlangra requires manufacturing skills that only a few craftsmen have. The rawthing bamboo is used because of the resistance of the thin strip of this bamboo to impact loads. The strips from the mat are cut from green bamboo, one set from the outer layer and the other from the inner layer. The two thick strips used for the trim are also cut bent and tied into the required triangular shape. All the strips are thoroughly dried before making the thlangra so that there is no shrinkage later.

Mathematical Components: Triangle

Pedagogical Implications: The Winnowing tray is very relevant and it can apply to the teaching-learning triangle since it is triangular. It can also be used for calculating the area of a triangle.

Application in the Teaching-Learning of Mathematics:

1. Model of triangle applicable in real life.
2. Calculating the area of a triangle.

FORTY-NINE
TUITHAWL (MIZO WATER GALLON)

Tuithawl

Indigenous Name: Tuithawl

About: Tuithawl is a Mizo water Gallon and is made from a bottled gourd. It has a circular opening for the intake and outlet of water and has a spherical body that can contain water. Mizo's are hard-working people in cultivating and crops growing. The daily routine in those days was to take care of the crops and the only available material for carrying water was the Water Gallon which was very useful in those days.

Mathematical Components: Circle, Sphere.

Pedagogical Implications: This material can be useful for demonstrating the different aspects of a sphere. It represents the three-dimensional shape and can be treated as a working model. It has a circular opening for intake and a spherical body. It will be applicable in a teaching circle and sphere.

Application in the Teaching-Learning of Mathematics:

1. Calculation of curved surface area and volume
2. Combination of sphere and circle.
3. Demonstrating circle.

FIFTY

Tuiumdar (A String Musical Instrument)

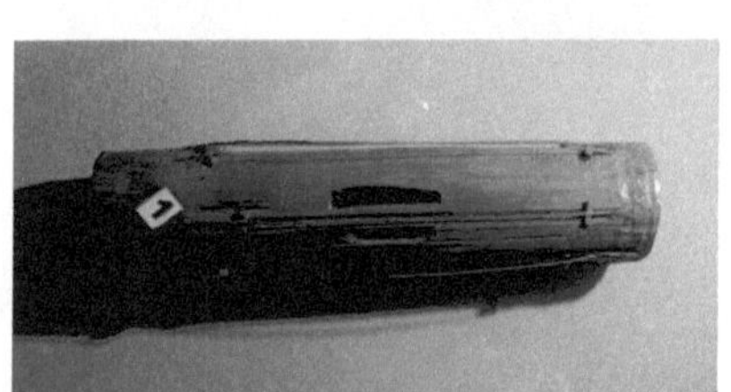

Tuiumdar

Indigenous Name: Tuiumdar

About: Tuiumdar is a Mizo traditional musical instrument made from bamboo. Bamboo was cut between the nodes forming a hollow cylinder. The bamboo itself provides a string (small bamboo stripes) and there is an opening for sound waves to travel in and out that makes the musical notes.

Mathematical Components: Hallow Cylinder.

Pedagogical Implications: Tuiumdar is a hollow cylinder and can be used for demonstrating a hollow cylinder. It can also be used for computing the lateral surface area of a cylinder.

Application in the Teaching-Learning of Mathematics:

1. Model of a cylinder.
2. Calculating the curved surface area of a cylinder.

FIFTY-ONE

Tuthlawh (A Hoe or Agricultural Implements)

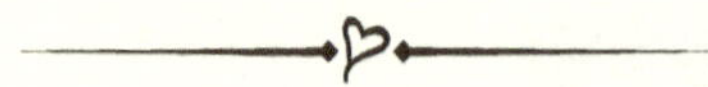

Tuthlawh

Indigenous Name: Tuthlawh

About: A Hoe is a traditional tool of Mizo used for cleaning the garden and surroundings. It has a triangular head made from metal and a long bamboo handle. It can also be used for shoveling, digging, stirring, etc.

Mathematical Components: Cylinder, triangle.

Pedagogical Implications: A hoe can be used for explaining cylinders, and triangles. The bamboo handle is cylindrical and can be used for calculating the volume and surface of a cylinder. The head can also be used for explaining triangles and a curve.

Application in the Teaching-Learning of Mathematics:

1. Model of a cylinder
2. Model of triangle and curve.
3. Calculating the volume and surface area of a cylinder.

FIFTY-TWO

VAIBEL (SMOKING PIPE)

Vaibel

Indigenous Name: Vaibel

About: It is a Mizo smoking pipe made from Bamboo. It was very common for the elders and used to smoke using Smoking pipes. A small hollow cylindrical bamboo was used for the pipe and a bigger cylinder was used for the container. It is a combination of two cylinders of different height and radius. It can also be mentioned that the material is purely cylindrical.

Mathematical Components: Hallow Cylinder, Circle, Cylinder

Pedagogical Implications: A smoking pipe can be used for demonstrating a cylinder. It can also be used for calculating the volume and surface area of a cylinder.

Application in the Teaching-Learning of Mathematics:

1. Model of a cylinder.
2. Model of a hollow cylinder.
3. Calculating the volume and surface area of a cylinder.

FIFTY-THREE

Zubel/Nganbel (Traditional Ceramic Jar)

Zubel/Nganbel

Indigenous Name: Zubel

About: Mizoram is famous for its traditional beer known as zu. It is prepared by fermenting rice, millet, or maize, and the container used for keeping this is called zubel. The local clay maker used to make it from clay with circular openings and having oval shapes bodies. Also, they used to make two handles and used to decorate the body in a diamond-cutting shape using bamboo stripes. It is very useful for keeping and carrying the zu (wine) in the Mizo society.

Mathematical Components: Circle, Oval.

Pedagogical Implications: This type of object can be used in teaching a lesson on circles and for explaining oval shapes. The oval shape can be somehow confusing for the learner, especially in lower classes. By showing the above materials, it is believed that the learner can have a clear-cut idea of how an oval looks (visualizing the structural aspects of an oval). Also, it has a circular opening that can be used for explaining a circle and for countering the circumference and area of a circle.

Application in the Teaching-Learning of Mathematics:

1. Model of oval shape.
2. Finding the area and perimeter of a circle.

FIFTY-FOUR
ZU NO (BEER CUP)

Zu No

Indigenous Name: Zu No

About: Zu no is a beer cup used for drinking Mizo traditional beer. It basically originates from Myanmar and is mostly used in the Mizo society for drinking liquor. It is small in size and very handy to handle in one palm. This cup seems to be an ideal hemispherical small bowl that can be very useful while teaching the hemisphere and its related aspects in mathematics at the elementary level.

Mathematical Components: Circle, Hemisphere.

Pedagogical Implications: It can be used for demonstrating circles and hemispheres. Also, it can be used for countering the volume and surface area of a hemisphere. The circular opening can be used to explain the circumference and area of the circle.

Application in the Teaching-Learning of Mathematics:

1. Computing the volume, curved and whole surface area of the hemisphere.
2. Countering the circumference and area of a circle.
3. Combining the different kinds of geometrical figures and making a meaningful shape.

References

- Aichele, D., & Downing, C. (1985). Increasing the Participation of Native Americans in Higher Mathematics. The National Science Foundation.
- Amit, M., & Abu Qouder, F. A. (2017). Weaving Culture and Mathematics in the Classroom: The Case of Bedouin Ethnomathematics. In M. Rosa et al. (Eds.), Ethnomathematics and Its Diverse Approaches for Mathematics Education. ICME-13 Monographs (pp. 23-50). Springer. https://doi.org/10.1007/978-3-319-59220-6_2
- Amit, M., Fried, M. N., & Abu-Naja, M. (2007). The Mathematics Club for Excellent Students as Common Ground for Bedouin and Other Israeli Youth. The Montana Mathematics Enthusiast, Monograph, 1, 75-90.
- Barton, B. (1996). Ethnomathematics: Exploring Cultural Diversity in Mathematics. Ph.D. Thesis, University of Auckland.
- Borba, M. C. (1997). Ethnomathematics and Education. In A. B. Powell, & M. Frankenstein (Eds.), Ethnomathematics: Challenging Eurocentrism in Mathematics Education (pp. 261-272). State University of New York Press.
- D'Ambrosio, U. (1984). Socio-Cultural Basis of Mathematics Education. In The Fifth International Congress on Mathematical. Adelaide Australia.
- D'Ambrosio, U. (1985). Ethnomathematics and Its Place in the History and Pedagogy of Mathematics. For the Learning of Mathematics, 5, 44-48.
- D'Ambrosio, U. (1990). Etnomatemática

[Ethnomathematics]. Editora ática.
- D'Ambrosio, U. (1993). Etnomatemática: Um Programa [Ethnomathematics: A Program]. A Educacao Matemática em Revista, 1, 5-11.
- D'Ambrosio, U. (2002). Ethnomathemathematics: An Overview. In M. de Monteiro (Ed.), Proceedings of Second International Conference on Ethnomathemathematics (pp 3-5). Lyrium Comunacacao Ltda.
- D'Ambrosio, U. (2006). Ethnomathematics: Link between Traditions and Modernity. ZDM, 40, 1033-1034. https://doi.org/10.1007/s11858-008-0163-3
- D'Ambrosio, U. (1987). Reflections on Ethnomathemathematics. International Study Group on Ethnomathemathematics. Newsletter, 3, 3-5.

About Authors

Dr. Prateek Chaurasia

Dr. Prateek Chaurasia is working as an assistant professor, in the Department of Education, Mizoram University. He has also served at the Regional Institute of Education, NCERT, Bhopal, M. P. as an assistant professor. Dr. Chaurasia has completed his Master in Education (M.Ed.) from the Regional Institute of Education, NCERT, Ajmer, Rajasthan and is a recipient of a Gold medal in M.Ed. He has obtained his Ph.D. from Banaras Hindu University, Varanasi, Uttar Pradesh. He is a recipient of prestigious fellowships like the UGC junior research fellowship & NCERT Doctoral Fellowship. He is working in the field of mathematics education, educational technology and assessment in education. He has published many research articles in national and international journals of repute. He is leading the major and minor research projects funded by premium institutions like ICSSR, Mizoram University and the Regional Institute of Education. He has also contributed to various government projects in the capacity of resource person.

TBC Lalramnghaka

TBC Lalramnghaka is a Research scholar in the Department of Education, Mizoram University. TBC has served for nearly eight years in the High School as a Mathematics teacher. Presently, he is working in the field of mathematics education. He is closely associated with the ethnomathematics and culturally responsive approach to mathematics learning.

www.ingramcontent.com/pod-product-compliance
Lightning Source LLC
Chambersburg PA
CBHW062219150726
47991CB00006B/2345